CLASSIC TRACKS

The World's Greatest Drummers Note For Note!

By Joe Bergamini
Foreword by Dom Famularo

Edited by William F. Miller
Design and layout by Michele M. Newhouse

ISBN 0-634-05168-7

Published by
Modern Drummer Publications, Inc.
12 Old Bridge Road
Cedar Grove, NJ 07009 USA

Contents

by Dom Famularo

During my global travels, when I first met Joe Bergamini at one of my events, he impressed me with his obvious enthusiasm for drumming. This began a long, ongoing relationship between the two of us. Joe studied with me for about five years, and I saw tangible results by a willing student not afraid of hard work. I then sent Joe to teaching legends Al Miller and Jim Chapin to learn how to analyze the past and current legends. (This undoubtedly planted the seeds for *MD Classic Tracks*.)

From the start, Joe's musical talent was strong, and he demonstrated dedication, perseverance, and humility all fueled by a deep passion for the instrument. Joe accepted any challenge I gave him. Our relationship has grown to collaborating on a technique book, *It's Your Move*, with many more books planned for the future.

As a teacher himself, Joe's constantly full schedule is the result of his commitment to his students and the excellent standards he sets. His band 4Front is another example of his passion for music. Three albums later, he actively performs and records within and without the group, filling his insane schedule.

I am proud and inspired by Joe's work on this project to document these great artists. I have used transcriptions in my "learning curve" for years. This collection has proven to be a huge aid in understanding these artists' thoughts and musical processes.

The drummers included in this book should be studied at great length. These songs are important to learn from, and these transcriptions are designed to guide you and challenge your playing. Studying them will allow you to stand on the shoulders of these players and look further, hopefully pushing the art form to the next level. Accept your responsibility to develop your talent and lead the way for *tomorrow's* greats.

Dom Famularo

Don Famularo is known as "Drumming's Global Ambassador." He is the author of two works: a motivational book called The Cycle Of Self-Empowerment, *and a drum technique book,* It's Your Move. *Find out more by visiting www.domfamularo.com.*

INTRODUCTION

From the earliest days of my experience with the drums, I've always listened to my favorite albums and tried to learn exactly what my idols were doing. This process not only made me a better listener, it made me a better *musician*. By doing this I was able to learn the patterns I heard on those albums, which expanded my playing in every possible direction: grooves, fills, coordination concepts, and more. It also helped my development because, after learning this material, I started to analyze the context, listen to the arrangement, and think about why the drummer might have chosen to play what he played.

This listening process continues for me to this day; I still find it exciting to put on an unfamiliar album and hear some great drumming that I can learn something from. The intention of this book is to help drummers with this great way of learning about music.

MD Classic Tracks is designed as a reference, a learning tool for the contemporary drummer. It contains transcriptions of thirteen tracks recorded by some of the most important contemporary drummers in rock and fusion. In these pages you'll find the exact drum parts recorded on tracks that drummers have been inspired by since their release.

Put on the CDs and listen along. Analyze the arrangements of the song, the grooves, the fills, the concepts, and the wonderful personalities emerging from these parts. It's my hope that listening to and learning these parts, combined with a regular regimen of drumming practice and lessons, will improve your reading, chops, and understanding of musical form. It will also make you intimately familiar with the playing of the thirteen drummers who most shaped *my* consciousness of the drumset.

I also hope that this book will serve as somewhat of a "historical document," cataloging thirteen classic albums from important musicians. If you use these as a starting point, and seek out more music from the same drummers and the other musicians on these recordings, you'll discover endless hours of inspiration.

I'd like to say a word about the artists we chose and why. An undertaking like this book is a very personal one. If you asked a jazz drummer to assemble a collection of "classic tracks," he'd probably come up with a list including Tony Williams, Elvin Jones, Buddy Rich, Max Roach, Papa Jo Jones, and many others. A funk drummer would probably choose Bernard Purdie, Harvey Mason, David Garibaldi, Clyde Stubblefield, and John "Jabo" Starks, among others.

I grew up with—and continue to love the playing of—the thirteen drummers covered herein. To me, they are among the most inspirational and important in modern music. This is not meant to be a "top-thirteen drummers" list; there were many players who were omitted only after long and careful consideration. Another author could easily come up with twenty more players equally worthy of inclusion.

Choosing the particular tracks was no easy task, either, with so many great ones available. We tried to settle on the "must know" tunes from certain drummers—for example, Jeff Porcaro's "Rosanna," Steve Gadd's "Late In The Evening," and Simon Phillips' "Space Boogie." To a huge fan of these three men, there are *many* tunes that spring to mind. But these particular songs represent these drummers so well that they seemed obvious choices.

For most of the other players represented here, we tried to pick tracks that displayed many of their signature concepts, rather than simply their best-known tunes. A good example is "Driven To Tears" from The Police, with Stewart Copeland on drums. While not their most famous song, it contains a great drum part with lots of the nuances Stewart is known for. I think this criteria holds true for most of the other songs. For example, some Vinnie Colaiuta fans may be surprised that I didn't transcribe a Frank Zappa tune. But "I'm Tweeked," from the drummer's self-titled solo album, contains all of what I love about Vinnie's playing in one place.

Another factor that determined the song selection was whether transcriptions of their work are already available in existing books and back issues of *Modern Drummer*. We simply didn't want to repeat a chart that's already available. To our knowledge, all of these tracks are appearing in print for the first time.

Joe Bergamini

ACKNOWLEDGEMENTS

I want to give a word of thanks to Bill Miller at Modern Drummer Publications, my able editor, a great drummer, and wonderful guy to work with. Thanks go also to *Modern Drummer* publisher Ron Spagnardi for his confidence in me about this project (and for giving me something to look forward to every month since I was thirteen!); Dom Famularo, who will always be my teacher and guide (and thanks for the foreword, Dom!); everyone at Sabian, Tama, Vic Firth, LP, XL Specialty, HQ Percussion, and Ritchie's Music Center; all my students; and everyone in the percussion industry who has encouraged and supported me. I'd also like to acknowledge my wonderful wife, Kim, for her constant support of my drumming career.

DEDICATION

To my parents, Ron and Millie, bigger heroes to me than any drummer could ever be.

NOTATION KEY

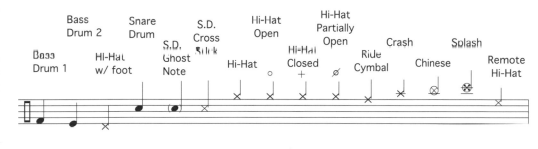

Other instruments notated on charts: Toms are notated per artist following the PAS Standard, using the following numbers of toms for each artist. (Although some players may use more than six toms, no more than this were needed to notate the songs.)

Three Toms—John Bonham
Four Toms—Steve Gadd, Vinnie Colaiuta, Jeff Porcaro, Stewart Copeland, Keith Moon, Terry Bozzio
Five Toms—Steve Smith
Six Toms—Carter Beauford, Phil Collins, Simon Phillips, Mike Portnoy, Neil Peart

JOHN BONHAM

John Bonham

"Out On The Tiles"
Led Zeppelin, *III* (Atlantic, 1970)

If there is one drumming legend whose playing is most misunderstood, it is probably John Bonham. Did he define modern rock drumming? Yes. Could the man play hard and loud? Yes. But what many rock drummers don't really appreciate is the *swing* that was present in everything he played. Coming from a jazz and rhythm & blues background, Bonham's swagger is the element of his playing that is almost impossible to duplicate. As with so many of the great players, it is crucially important to listen not only to what he chose to play, but *how he played it*.

"Out On The Tiles" hasn't appeared in print before, but it contains a classic drum part. First and foremost, check out the ambient, almost jazzy drum sound—often imitated, *never* duplicated. Next take a hard listen to the main groove and notice the slight inflections of swing. It would be impossible to put this on paper exactly as it sounds.

Regarding the drum part itself, the main groove contains lots of Bonzo's legendary footwork (check out the double strokes!) and snare-kick interplay. Listen to the ease with which he navigates the bar of 7/8. As the tune heads to its conclusion, John energizes the ride-out with lots of tasty fills over a driving ride and left-foot hi-hat pulse.

Jim Marshall

L.F. Hi-Hat continues simile

Fade...

KEITH MOON

Keith Moon
Keith Moon

"The Real Me"

The Who, *Quadrophenia* **(MCA, 1973)**

Many of the elements of nuance and touch that make a player sound unique cannot be put on paper. This holds true for no one like it does for The Who's Keith Moon, whose wild abandon and sheer uncontrolled insanity on the drums will never see an equal. While most of the players in this book possess the ultimate in control, Keith Moon sounds like he is a nanosecond away from complete *loss* of control and utter rhythmic meltdown. That's the beauty of his playing!

While all the above is true, a look over the chart for "The Real Me" reveals a structure even within the mind of this wildest of players. The verses generally stay on the hi-hat and contain little snare drum flourishes and groove variations. The choruses are where Moon lets loose with a rain of tom notes to punctuate Roger Daltrey's wailing vocal. As the song goes on, these fills get longer and more frequent. It truly is a fascinating exercise to look at Keith Moon's playing on paper.

Drum wisdom says "play every song like it might be your last." Keith Moon certainly sounds like he accomplished this.

Ride played crash-style:

PHIL COLLINS

Phil Collins

"Dance On A Volcano"
Genesis, *A Trick Of The Tail* (Atco, 1975)

Genesis began as one of the premier art rock groups of the mid-'70s, became one of the cutting-edge progressive rock bands at the turn of the decade, and morphed into a phenomenally successful pop act in the '80s. At the helm for most of this adventure was a tremendously talented musician named Phil Collins. Although he is now known as a Grammy-winning singer/songwriter, Phil's true fans know that his drumming is just as inspirational.

"Dance On A Volcano" is a great example of Phil's playing. This tune clearly demonstrates Phil's ability to traverse difficult arrangements and time changes smoothly and with incomparable groove. Even though this is fairly early on in his career, Phil's signature tom sound is on full display here, along with his tasty use of the hi-hat.

Most of this song is in 7/8, but Phil plays various feels within the seven, sometimes phrasing it 4-3 and sometimes 3-4. He mixes these variations deftly while never losing the forward motion of the song. The main verse is particularly interesting—a driving bass drum pulse with the snare and hi-hat accenting the "&" of beat 6. Now *that's* original. Pay attention to how Phil phrases and places his fills, his choice of sounds and colors on the kit, and how he builds the intensity with more ghost notes and thicker phrasing as the song develops.

Anne Fishbein

Helene Glassman

STEVE GADD

Steve Gadd

"Late In The Evening"
Paul Simon, *One-Trick Pony* (Warner Bros., 1980)

Attempting to pick a single song to analyze by the great Steve Gadd is an exercise in futility. Steve has played on so many legendary tracks with so many artists that it's easy to see why he is considered one of the greatest drummers to ever touch a pair of sticks. "Late In The Evening," by Paul Simon, is a simple pop tune that has been elevated to classic status with one of the must-know grooves of the modern drumset.

The groove is based on the Afro-Caribbean mozambique. The pattern played on the rim and cowbell is heard in the folkloric drumming of that style. Although accents are not written in, the rim figure follows the basic accent inflection of traditional mozambique, so listen to it carefully. The toms play a counter-melody to this pattern, which can take a little practice to line up, and the bass drum and hi-hat anchor the time with a driving quarter-note pulse.

Steve recorded the song holding two sticks side-by-side in each hand—the sound of the sticks hitting together in the hand and flamming on the rim thickens up the groove and adds a "percussion section" effect.

Ebet Roberts

Veryl Oakland

(Note: entire song played with two sticks in each hand.)
R.H. on rim of floor tom:

Horn melody

STEWART COPELAND
Stewart Copeland
Stewart Copeland

"Driven To Tears"
The Police, *Zenyatta Mondatta* (A&M, 1980)

Stewart Copeland's influence in contemporary pop drumming is undeniable. As many of the rock musicians who grew up in the '80s begin to make records of their own, Stewart's name comes up constantly as a major influence across the spectrum of pop, rock, punk, ska, and fusion. His is a unique voice; you can analyze this chart and play every note as it is written, but you'll never sound like Stewart. His inflection and touch are among the most sophisticated and individual in all of drumming. And his creativity and energy are there to match.

This selection, as with many others in this book, was chosen for the way it showcases many of the key traits of the drummer. In "Driven To Tears," you'll immediately hear Stewart's masterly use of accents to color parts, both on the hi-hat and on the ride cymbal. By breaking up the placement of notes and accents, Copeland adds variety and a sense of urgency to the driving 4/4 ska bass drum pulse underneath. The cross-stick on the snare is another signature of Stewart's, coming from his experience with reggae.

Notice how the chorus switches to a half-time backbeat on the snare, with all kinds of little accents and toys coloring the groove. Listen for the splashes, Octobans, and toms, all used with the utmost degree of musicality. Also note Stewart's mastery of the hi-hat. Along with the accents mentioned above, pay attention to the way he uses various rhythms and degrees of tightness—from clamped tightly shut to wide open—to get the most out of this instrument.

Alex Solca

Ebet Roberts

Octoban:

(Slight accents on R.C.)

SIMON PHILLIPS

Simon Phillips

"Space Boogie"
Jeff Beck, *There And Back* (Epic, 1980)

Simon Phillips is unique among drummers. He's a graceful powerhouse, a musician attuned to the finest nuances of his sound and touch, yet able to drive the biggest rock bands in the world. Playing open-handed on his massive kit, Simon gets his drums to sing like no one else. His energy and consistent ability to come up with unique and dazzling drum parts are unmatched. In recent years Simon has displayed his versatility and true musical mastery in a wide variety of styles, from his own modern fusion band, to bebop (Vantage Point), to classic fusion (Doves Of Fire), to pop (replacing the late, great Jeff Porcaro in Toto).

"Space Boogie" truly deserves the title "classic track." It's taken from Jeff Beck's 1980 album *There And Back*, and it features a blindingly fast double bass drum shuffle—*in seven*, no less. Aside from the speed, what makes this groove difficult is the placement of many ghost notes in the measure, some of which overlap the ride cymbal part. Practice this groove very slowly at first. It is very important to keep the ghost notes soft.

Little else need be said about the chart other than the fact that it is a high-level challenge to any drummer's speed, endurance, and timing. Besides all of that, it's full of insanely fast and energetic drum fills—courtesy of one of the giants of modern drumming, Simon Phillips.

Alex Solca

courtesy Tama/Hoshino Gakki

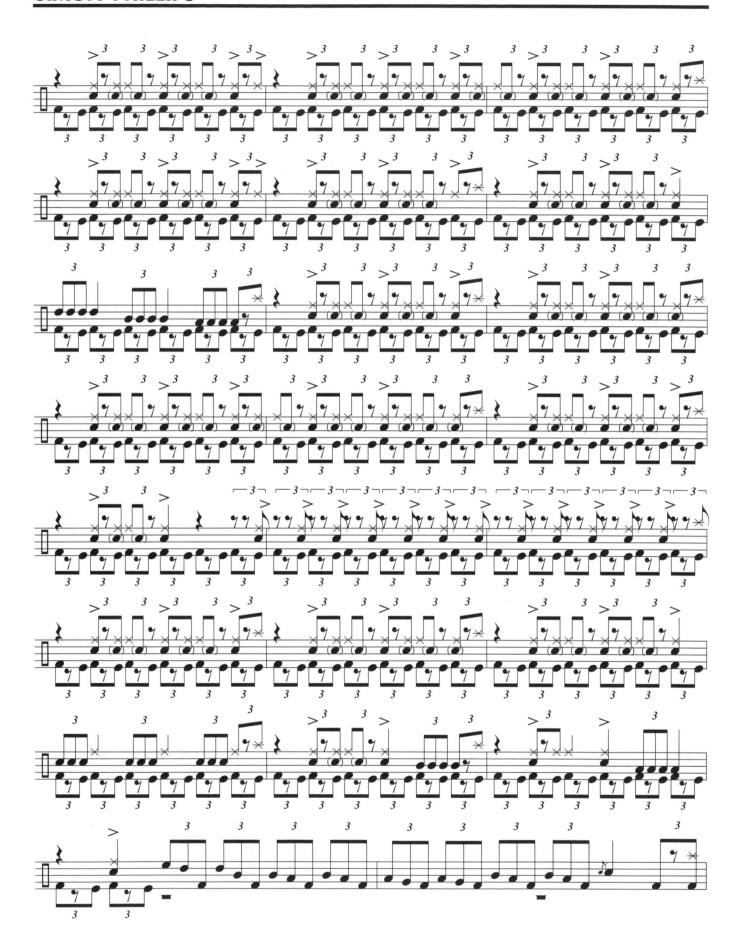

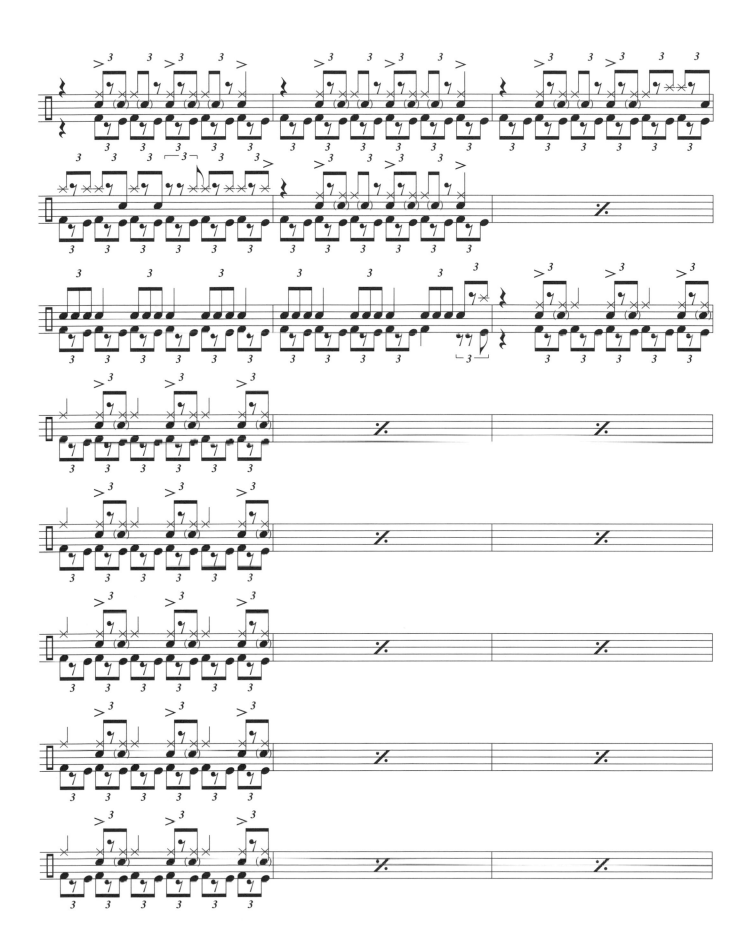

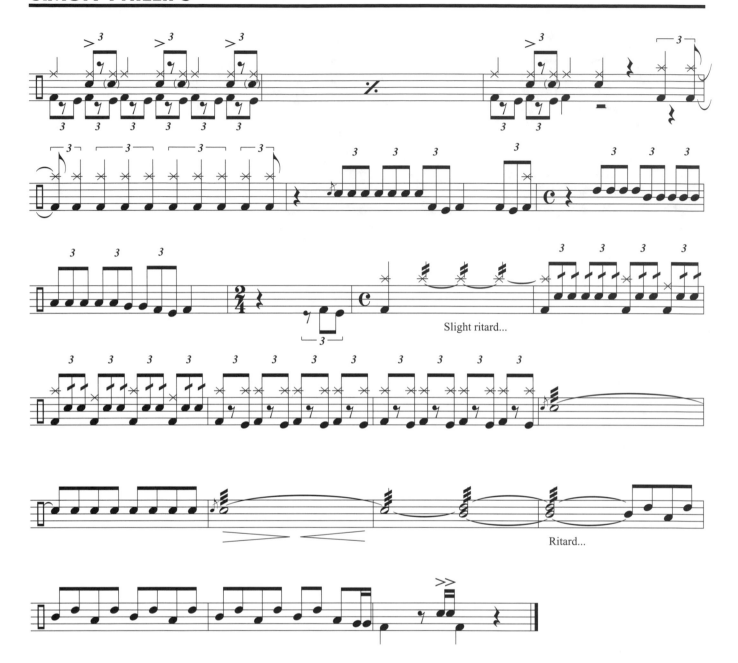

NEIL PEART
Neil Peart

"The Camera Eye"
Rush, *Moving Pictures* (Mercury, 1981)

Neil Peart is revered among rock fans more than any other drummer, and for good reason. His parts transcend the concept of simply "fitting the song." Rather, they become one with the composition, so that they are an inseparable part of every Rush song. It's hard to think of any other drummer who has 20,000 people air drumming along to every note he plays at each concert! Add to that Peart's creativity both in his playing and in his use of technology, and the fact that he and Rush are constantly searching for new musical ground, and you'll certainly conclude that Neil is one of the most important drummers of the last twenty-five years.

As with many of the drummers in this book, it was quite difficult to pick one song to analyze. But "The Camera Eye," which hasn't appeared in print before, is an excellent choice, because it gives us a great opportunity to observe how Neil builds his part throughout a song, phrases odd times with ease, and adds the signature fills that work so well within the music.

The song starts with a wonderfully phrased rudimental section on the snare drum. (Check out the clean rolls and use of flams.) Then it develops into one of the many instrumental sections of the song. In these parts, listen for Neil's choice of tight or loose hi-hats or ride cymbal to give the proper backing. The solo drum fills that occur over the keyboard vamp are vintage Neil— powerful, creative, and appropriate. The softer verse sections feature a lighter drum groove that weaves through the odd meters and complements the vocals perfectly. There's also a double-handed riding section with hi-hat chokes, some wonderfully phrased two-bar fills, and plenty of energetic rock grooves.

Andrew MacNaughton

(Cr. 1st x only)

JEFF PORCARO

Jeff Porcaro Jeff Porcaro

"Rosanna"
Toto, *IV* (CBS, 1982)

The late Jeff Porcaro is one of the most recorded drummers in history, thanks to the depth of passion and groove that came out of every note he played. Jeff defined the LA studio musician—the master of groove and a consummate pro who could play anything. But his first love was his band Toto, and "Rosanna" is a classic rock track with an equally classic drum part. Like "Late In The Evening," this is a groove every drummer *must* learn at some point in his or her development.

The drum groove on "Rosanna" is a half-time shuffle, which means the backbeat comes on beat 3 of each measure. The most difficult thing about this groove is the correct placement and volume of the ghost notes on the snare drum. These notes (in parentheses) should be played about a half inch off the surface of the snare drum, so softly that they mix in with and resemble the sound of the hi-hat. It takes practice to achieve the correct effect. Listen to the recording of this song and notice the wide difference in volume between the backbeat (one of the loudest things in the mix) and the ghost notes (barely audible). The bass drum plays several variations against this throughout the tune.

The chorus is set up by a triplet run that ends on the last partial of the triplet on beat 2. This is often mis-played by bands covering this song, so listen to it carefully. Jeff's dynamics in the pre-chorus are another great example of his musicality.

Randy Bachman

Paul Jonason

Band enters

Keyboard Solo

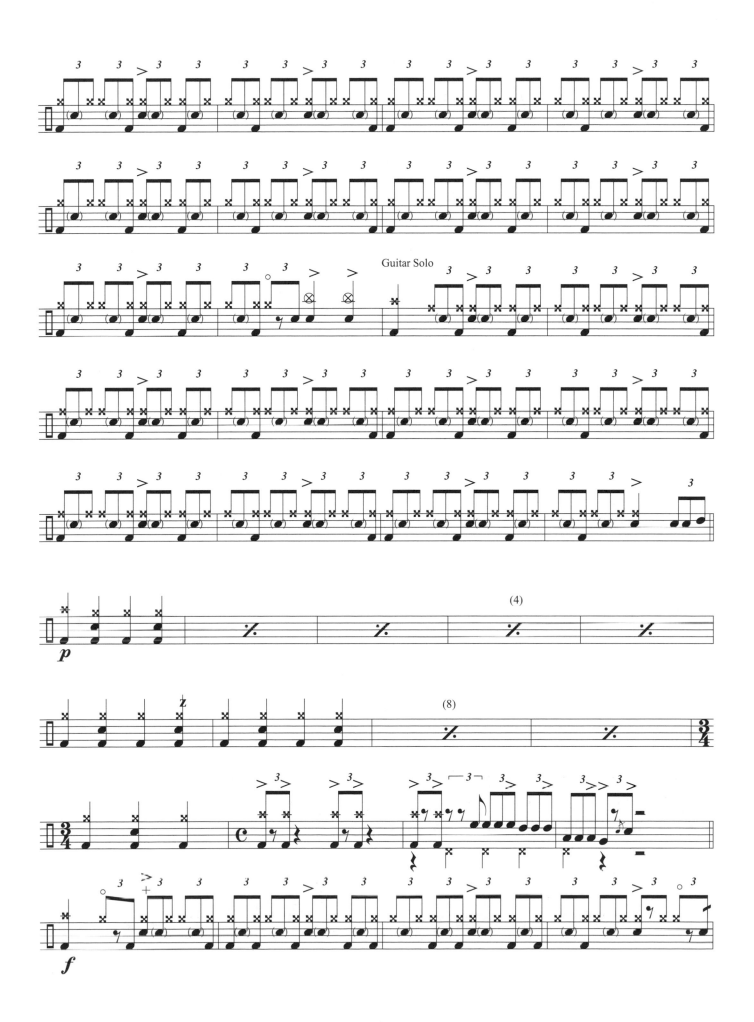

Guitar Solo

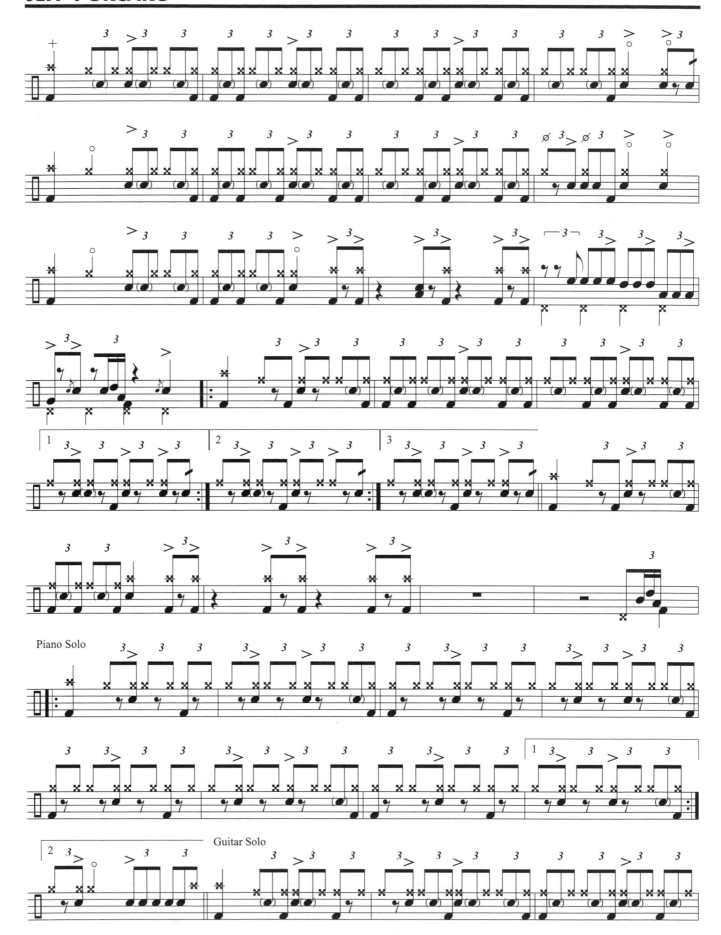

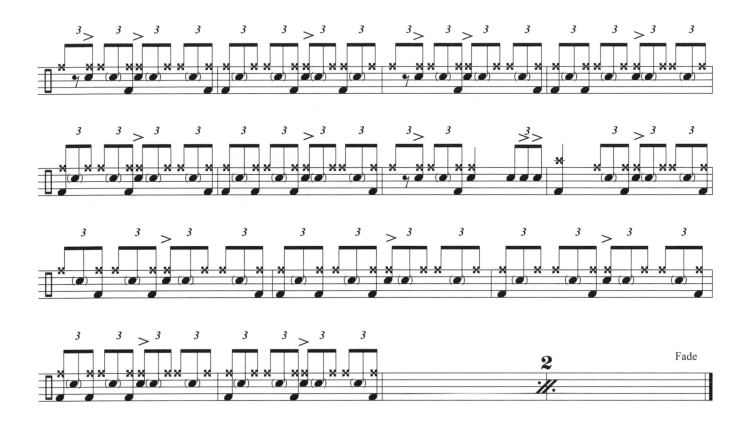

TERRY BOZZIO

Terry Bozzio

"Sling Shot"
Jeff Beck, *Guitar Shop* **(Epic, 1989)**

Terry Bozzio is widely considered the foremost drum soloist of our time. With a fully developed musical concept and a unique drum and cymbal setup to go with it, Terry is truly expanding the frontiers of the drumset. His work with Frank Zappa, UK, Jeff Beck, Missing Persons, and others was already enough to garner him a place in drumming history. But his achievement of being the first player to perform solo *drum music* concerts guarantees it. Terry's also an incredible team player, and a listen back to 1989's "Sling Shot" hints at some of what was to come in his playing.

Probably the most obvious Terry signature here is the varied choice of riding surfaces he uses to color the arrangement. A short, sharp Chinese sound here accents key ensemble rhythms, while the main hi-hat handles the tune's A sections. On the B section, Terry punctuates accents on a noticeably different-sounding Chinese cymbal, generating a nasty sense of excitement. Later he moves to the floor tom to drive home the end of the tune.

The four-bar drum break at the end has a manic sense of unbalance, as Terry introduces triplets for the first time in the duple-pulsed tune, then modulates to 16ths as he flashes through some of his signature hand-foot combinations. This brings a perfectly conceived and executed drum part to a conclusion.

Alex Solca

Note: In this song, all snare and crash notes are assumed to be accents.
Also note the use of a second China cymbal.

(2nd China Cym:)

VINNIE COLAIUTA

Vinnie Colaiuta

"I'm Tweeked"
Vinnie Colaiuta (Stretch, 1994)

Vinnie Colaiuta is held in the highest esteem by drummers, and is considered a true genius of the instrument. "I'm Tweeked," from his self-titled 1994 solo album, shows the amazing mind of a master at work. According to interviews with Vinnie, the tune was based around a drum loop he was playing around with, when he decided to move the apparent downbeats around in the phrase. "Apparent" is the appropriate term, because the main part of the song stays in 4/4 but the drums create the illusion of a new measure by displacing the accent by a 16th note. This causes the bizarre "hiccups" in the time, and, as Vinnie says, "Who could dance to that?"

Other things to watch for in this tune are the utterly amazing inventions of fills and variations Vinnie places into the driving backbeat groove of the tune, as well as the double-pedal flourishes that he throws in. There are two breaks in the song where the drums rest, and the keyboards superimpose a grouping of seven over the 4/4 pulse. To bring the band back in after this, Vinnie plays lightning-fast single strokes from pianissimo to forte. His control is astounding. The second time this part occurs, he plays alternating 32nds between snare and bass drum! Keep shedding, kids, this might take a while.

The drum solo occurs over a vamp in three (listen to the keyboards and bass, and you'll hear the three) and contains classic examples of the phrasing, chops, musicality, and inventiveness that have made this man an idol among drummers.

Alex Solca

Lissa Wales

Guitar enters:

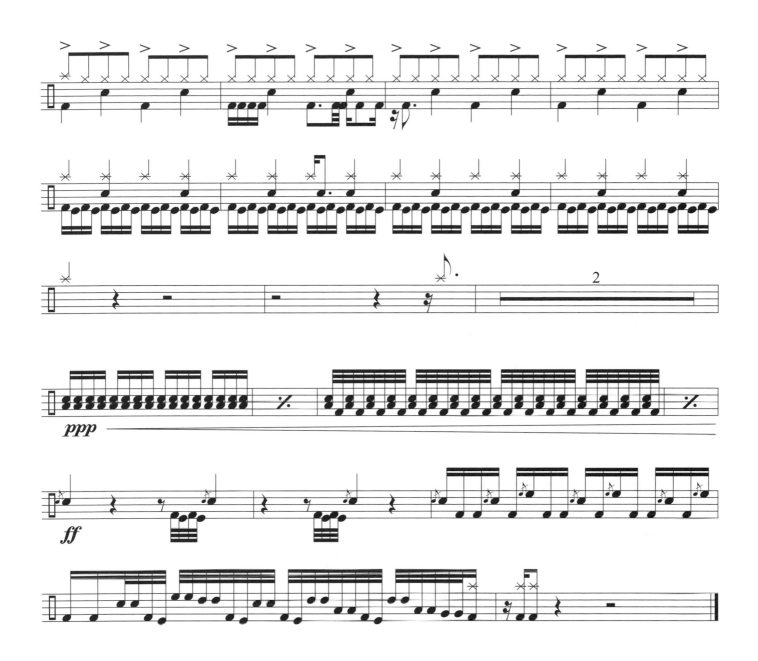

MIKE PORTNOY

Mike Portnoy

"6:00"

Dream Theater, *Awake* (Eastwest, 1994)

One of the younger players covered in this book, Mike Portnoy grew up listening to most of the others. Mike has taken ideas from them all, combined them with a deep passion for Zappa-style complexity and a penchant for heavy metal, and has emerged as the drum hero of the 2000s. Portnoy's chops are undeniable, but what's more impressive is his *memory*. Try playing along to a Dream Theater arrangement and you'll see why.

Dream Theater's "6:00" is a potpourri of drum concepts, from a mind that is obviously overflowing with ideas. The solo drum intro establishes the linear, broken-16th-note groove that drives most of the song. Throughout, you'll hear 32nd-note flourishes on the hi-hat and well-placed punctuations on splashes and Chinese cymbals.

A major drummer's double-take occurs after the first 6/8 part, where Mike launches into the burning double-bass 32nds that occur under the spoken-word verse. Rewind that bit a few times and check out how even it is. (And this was recorded pre-Pro Tools!)

Robert W. Fritsch

Icebell:

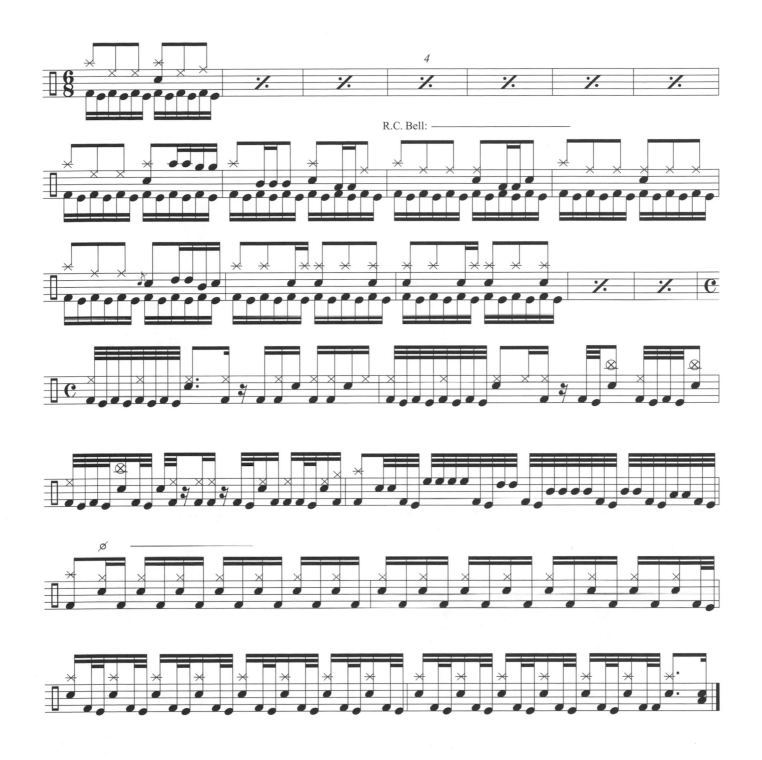

R.C. Bell: ⎯⎯⎯⎯⎯⎯⎯⎯⎯⎯⎯⎯⎯⎯⎯

STEVE SMITH

Steve Smith

"One More"
Journey, *Trial By Fire* (Columbia, 1996)

Steve Smith is consistently voted one of the best all-around drummers in the world, and for those who know his playing, it does seem that he can do it all. Between Journey and Vital Information, Smith covers more ground than most players do in a lifetime, and that's not to mention the many recordings he's made with other artists in styles from jazz to pop to fusion. Steve's a historian of the instrument, and his playing reflects the depth of a master musician.

"One More," from Journey's *Trial By Fire* album, is a great listen for drummers. After Steve left Journey, where he recorded some of pop music's signature drum tracks, his playing level rose to the stratosphere both technically and musically as he pursued many projects. This track shows him returning to Journey as a man on top of his game, playing a totally driving, grooving, creative, and exciting drum part. Nary a note can be added or taken away.

The way Steve drives the time on his hi-hats, and the definition of his bass drum, are enough to let you know that he's in total control. The broken double bass drum pattern in the chorus is one of those ideas that fits so perfectly, it seems immediately familiar, as it drives the energy of the tune to the next level. Listen to the cleanliness of the overlapping notes played by snare and kick. Two or three of the fills, including the monstrous hand-foot interchange at the end of the song, serve to briefly reveal the monster concealed behind the kit on this track.

Steve with Journey in 1983.

Ebet Roberts

Note: Hi-hat parts are played on
trashy-sounding remote closed hats.

Keyboard Intro

CARTER BEAUFORD

Carter Beauford

"Tripping Billies"
Dave Matthews Band, *Crash* (RCA, 1996)

Carter Beauford's playing with The Dave Matthews Band combines elements of rock, funk, and fusion into a powerfully creative and exciting style. Playing open-handed (with his left hand on the ride), Carter incorporates the colorful elements of his large kit into his playing in very creative ways. When playing live, Carter is always in the moment, improvising and pushing the envelope in ways that compare to the greatest of the jazz-fusion players—yet he manages to make it work in the context of an incredibly popular rock band.

"Tripping Billies" contains many of Carter's signature elements. His open-handed style allows him to play the hi-hat without crossing his hands, which leads to many creative possibilities in his grooves.

You'll notice that in this song, as in most DMB tunes, Carter rarely lets the hi-hat settle into a repetitive pattern. He varies its rhythms and adds all kinds of embellishments, often leaving the snare voice by itself (i.e., not playing the hi-hat and snare together). Also check out Carter's use of the splash cymbal as a riding device in this song.

The song opens with some ensemble hits, which leave Carter ample space to solo around. He fills these spaces tastefully, using the various voices of his kit to create a very interesting and funky tapestry of colors. Note Carter's use of the left-foot hi-hat to punctuate his ideas. These same figures occur before the guitar solo and again at the end of the song, and Carter builds the intensity for each section.

THE MODERN DRUMMER LIBRARY

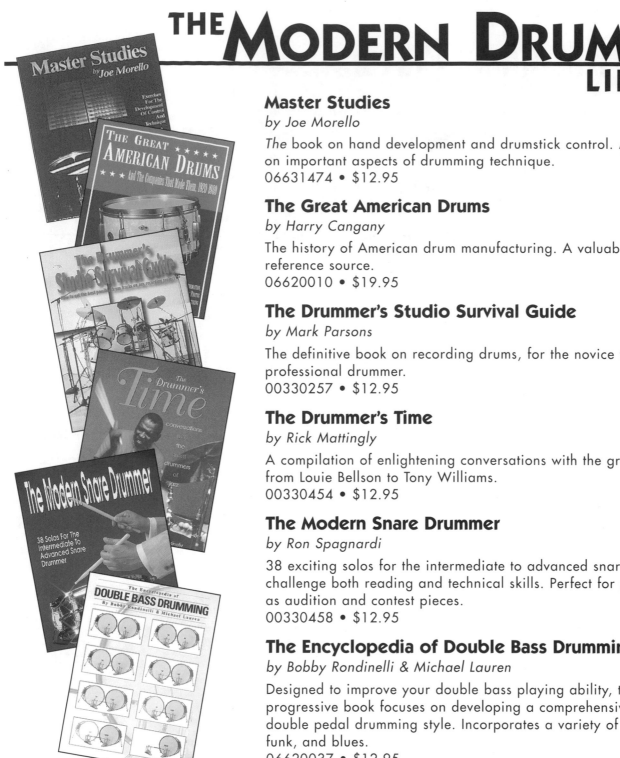

Master Studies
by Joe Morello

The book on hand development and drumstick control. *Master Studies* focuses on important aspects of drumming technique.
06631474 • $12.95

The Great American Drums
by Harry Cangany

The history of American drum manufacturing. A valuable collector's reference source.
06620010 • $19.95

The Drummer's Studio Survival Guide
by Mark Parsons

The definitive book on recording drums, for the novice to professional drummer.
00330257 • $12.95

The Drummer's Time
by Rick Mattingly

A compilation of enlightening conversations with the great drummers of jazz, from Louie Bellson to Tony Williams.
00330454 • $12.95

The Modern Snare Drummer
by Ron Spagnardi

38 exciting solos for the intermediate to advanced snare drummer that challenge both reading and technical skills. Perfect for percussion majors and as audition and contest pieces.
00330458 • $12.95

The Encyclopedia of Double Bass Drumming
by Bobby Rondinelli & Michael Lauren

Designed to improve your double bass playing ability, this progressive book focuses on developing a comprehensive double bass drum or double pedal drumming style. Incorporates a variety of styles including rock, funk, and blues.
06620037 • $12.95

Applied Rhythms 06630365 • $8.95	**Great Jazz Drummers** 06621755 • $19.95	**The New Breed** 06631619 • $12.95
Best of Concepts 06621766 • $9.95	**Electronic Drummer** 06631500 • $9.95	**The Working Drummer** 00330264 • $14.95
Best of Modern Drummer: Rock 06621759 • $9.95	**Progressive Independence** 00330290 • $12.95	**Cross-Sticking Studies** 00330377 • $12.95
When in Doubt, Roll 06630298 • $13.95	**Drum Wisdom** 06630510 • $7.95	

* Prices, contents and availability are subject to change without notice.

FOR MORE INFORMATION, SEE YOUR LOCAL MUSIC DEALER,
OR WRITE TO:

HAL•LEONARD®
CORPORATION
7777 W. BLUEMOUND RD. P.O. BOX 13819 MILWAUKEE, WI 53213
WWW.HALLEONARD.COM